By looking at art with children, you can help them develop their innate capacities for careful observation and creative imagination. Each picture in *Places* contains a defined setting. In addition, each features such elements as people, activities, particular times of day, seasons, and weather. Children can begin by naming different things they see. You can ask them how they recognize these things, and how each thing might relate to their own lives. You can also lead children to see more elements in each picture, and encourage them to imagine stories based on what their eyes tell them. There are notes at the back of the book to help.

Enjoy looking together!

W9-CNC-189

# Places

**Philip Yenawine**

**The Museum of Modern Art, New York**
**Delacorte Press**

Acknowledgments
This book was enriched by the contributions of Jessica Altholz,
Amelia Arenas, Harriet S. Bee, Riva Castleman, Peter Galassi, David Gale,
Abigail Housen, Nancy Miller, Carol Morgan, and the designers
Takaaki Matsumoto, Michael McGinn, and Mikio Sakai of M Plus M
Incorporated. I would also like to acknowledge Osa Brown,
Mikki Carpenter, Penny Cooper, Matthew Diehl, Barbara Greenberg,
George Nicholson, Edward Robinson, Rena Rosenwasser, Marc Sapir,
Richard Tooke, and Rebecca, Tad, and Patricia Yenawine. I am extremely
grateful to all of them.

Library of Congress Cataloging in Publication Data

Yenawine, Philip.
Places/Philip Yenawine.
p.  cm.
Summary:  Examines, in simple terms, the nature of imaginary and realis-
tic places created by such modern artists as Hopper, Munch, and Shahn.
1. Art—Themes, motives—Juvenile literature.  2. Art appreciation—
Juvenile literature.  3. The Museum of Modern Art (New York, N.Y.)—
Juvenile literature.[1. Art appreciation.  2. The Museum of Modern Art
(New York, N.Y.)]  I. Title.
N7560.Y46  1993
701'.1—dc20
92-11202
CIP
AC
ISBN 0-87070-173-8 (MoMA)
ISBN 0-385-30900-7 (Delacorte Press)

The Museum of Modern Art
11 West 53 Street
New York, NY 10019

Delacorte Press
Bantam Doubleday Dell Publishing Group, Inc.
1540 Broadway
New York, NY 10036

Printed in Italy

October 1993
10  9  8  7  6  5  4  3  2  1

# Looking at pictures, you can imagine practically any place.

Natalia Gontcharova. *The City Square.* 1914

# You can visit a town . . .

Joseph Pickett. *Manchester Valley.* 1914–18?

# or look around a farm.

Thomas Hart Benton. *Homestead*. 1934

# You can see yourself working . . .

Frances Benjamin Johnston. *Stairway of the Treasurer's Residence: Students at Work.* 1899–1900

**or playing. Which boys are playing and which are watching? Can you tell where they are?**

Ben Shahn. *Handball.* 1939

# Is this place in a city? How can you tell?
# What time of year do you think it is?

André Derain. *The Seine at Chatou.* 1906

# How can you tell where this man is?

Yasuo Kuniyoshi. *Self-Portrait as a Golf Player.* 1927

# Can you imagine being inside this room, dressed up and feeling very fancy?

Florine Stettheimer. *Family Portrait, II*. 1933

# Here is a very different kind of room. Can you describe it? What is happening here?

Jacob Lawrence. *The Migration of the Negro.* 1940–41

9

# Pictures can let you look through windows.
# What do you see outside?

Pierre Bonnard. *House in a Courtyard.* 1899

Fairfield Porter. *Flowers by the Sea.* 1965

# What do you think this woman sees outside her window?

Edward Hopper. *East Side Interior.* 1922

# Might she see a place like this?

## or this? Why do you think so?

Edward Hopper. *Gas.* 1940; Edward Hopper. *Corner Saloon.* 1913

# Pictures can make you think of stormy nights . . . of the rain and wind in your face.

Edvard Munch. *The Storm*. 1893

# In pictures, you can visit strange houses.

# What is happening in this place?

Antonio Lopez-Garcia. *The Apparition*. 1963

Imagine a world where bugs are huge.

Find butterflies and moths and other creatures you may never have seen before.

Can you find flowers, clouds, rocks, and water?

Odilon Redon. *Butterflies.* 1910

# Pictures can let you look up into trees, as mice might . . .

Gustav Klimt. *The Park*. 1910 or earlier

18

# or look down on houses and pathways, as birds can.

André Kertesz. *Touraine*. 1930

**If you flew above the city at night, it might look like a pattern of light.**

Berenice Abbott. *New York at Night.* 1933

# Here's another pattern.

# Can you imagine city blocks? streets? cars?

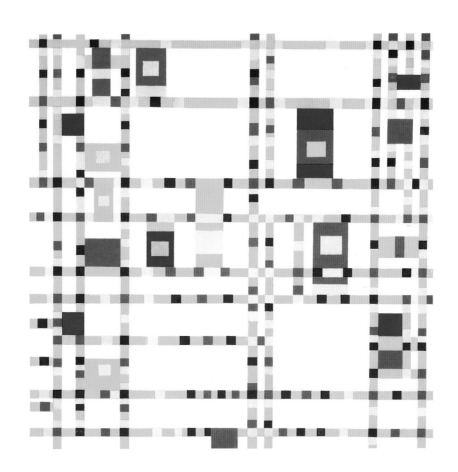

Piet Mondrian. *Broadway Boogie Woogie*. 1942–43

21

**Looking and imagining can help you think of things to draw. Can you draw what you see from your window? Can you draw the country and the city? places for work and play? real and made-up places? What other kinds of places can you think of?**

The art in this book is in the collection of The Museum of Modern Art in New York City, but you can find interesting pictures at any museum or gallery. You can also look for pictures and patterns in magazines, books, buildings, parks, and gardens.

Page 1

Natalia Gontcharova
*The City Square* (scenery design for the ballet *Le Coq d'Or*). 1914
Gouache, watercolor, and pencil on cardboard
18 3/8 x 24 1/4" (46.7 x 61.6 cm)
Acquired through the Lillie P. Bliss Bequest

There are dozens of details in this fanciful, colorful set design. Looking in windows and doors, finding animals, boats, flags, towers, and flowers is a great way to open a child's eyes.

Page 2

Joseph Pickett
*Manchester Valley*. 1914–18?
Oil with sand on canvas
45 1/2 x 60 5/8" (115.4 x 153.7 cm)
Gift of Abby Aldrich Rockefeller

This work by a self-taught artist has a simplicity that often appeals to children. Ask children to take an inventory of what's included in the picture, and ask them about the season and the weather.

Page 3

Thomas Hart Benton
*Homestead*. 1934
Tempera and oil on composition board
25 x 34" (63.5 x 86.4 cm)
Gift of Marshall Field (by exchange)

Benton is a master at depicting the American scene. Consider what the farmer might be doing at this moment. How about the pigs? Ask what might lie beyond the buildings.

Page 4

Frances Benjamin Johnston
*Stairway of the Treasurer's Residence: Students at Work*, from *The Hampton Institute Album*. 1899–1900
Platinum print
7 1/2 x 9 1/2" (19 x 24.1 cm)
Gift of Lincoln Kirstein

Though the six men pictured are hard at work, they seem to be posing. The angles of their bodies echo the stairway's structure, emphasizing lines and patterns as much as the activity depicted.

Page 5

Ben Shahn
*Handball*. 1939
Tempera on paper over composition board
22 3/4 x 31 1/4" (57.8 x 79.4 cm)
Abby Aldrich Rockefeller Fund

This picture seems less static than the last one. Children will have to look beyond the court to determine the location of this handball game. What about the season and weather?

Page 6

André Derain
*The Seine at Chatou*. 1906
Oil on canvas
29 1/8 x 48 3/4" (74 x 123.8 cm)
The William S. Paley Collection

We seem to be standing on a grassy riverbank, looking across the calm waters toward a town. The colors of a bright summer day are especially intense. The bare branches of the tree and saplings conveniently frame our view.

**Page 7**

Yasuo Kuniyoshi
*Self-Portrait as a Golf Player*. 1927
Oil on canvas
50 1/4 x 40 1/4" (127.6 x 102.2 cm)
Abby Aldrich Rockefeller Fund

Like Johnston's photograph, Kuniyoshi's self-portrait catches a figure frozen in an action. He seems to be posing, rather than playing golf. Look beyond the figure to the landscape and sky. Think about why the artist might have chosen to represent himself in this way.

**Page 8**

Florine Stettheimer
*Family Portrait, II*. 1933
Oil on canvas
46 1/4 x 64 5/8" (117.4 x 164 cm)
Gift of Miss Ettie Stettheimer

Despite overly large flowers that partially block our view, we can still see into a grand room in which there are four elegantly dressed women. You might point out the artist herself on the left, complete with palette, brushes, and high heels.

**Page 9**

Jacob Lawrence
*The Migration of the Negro*.
1940–41, from a series of 60 works (30 in the Museum's collection)
Tempera on gesso on composition board
18 x 12" (45.7 x 30.5 cm)
Gift of Mrs. David M. Levy

Panel 56: *Among the last groups to leave the South was the Negro professional who was forced to follow his clientele to make a living.*

Omitting most details, Lawrence shows a doctor at a patient's bedside, with his stethoscope and bag. He is framed within a triangle, which might represent the light from an unseen bulb overhead. The vertical division of the triangle may suggest the corner of a spare, darkened room. Look for differences between the rooms and people in this image and the one before.

**Page 10**

Pierre Bonnard
*House in a Courtyard* from the portfolio *Some Scenes of Parisian Life*. 1899
Lithograph, printed in color
13 11/16 x 10 1/4" (34.7 x 26 cm)
Larry Aldrich Fund (by exchange)

We see buildings, windows, and other architectural details here, but this image, framed by the window, might seem as much a design as a realistic depiction of a scene.

**Page 11**

Fairfield Porter
*Flowers by the Sea*. 1965
Oil on composition board
20 x 19 1/2" (50.6 x 49.5 cm)
Larry Aldrich Foundation Fund

The vertical and horizontal lines of the windows and their reflections on the tabletop create a sense of pattern, as in the Bonnard image. The vase of flowers and the suggestion of water and rocks evoke a pleasant sense of summer by the sea.

**Page 12**

Edward Hopper
*East Side Interior*. 1922
Etching, printed in black
7 7/8 x 9 13/16" (20 x 25 cm)
Gift of Abby Aldrich Rockefeller

Sitting at her sewing machine, leaning forward, one hand on the wheel, this young woman has been caught by a reverie, or perhaps by something she sees. She is completely absorbed. Note the porch column and railing outside the window.

**Page 13**

Edward Hopper
*Gas*. 1940
Oil on canvas
26 1/4 x 40 1/4" (66.7 x 102.2 cm)
Mrs. Simon Guggenheim Fund

Is there any evidence in the preceding picture that the woman might be looking out on this rustic highway scene? Children can try to guess the season and time of day. What might the man be doing, dressed as he is?